# My Hero

By

**Dawn Minall**

*This book is dedicated to Hero – without his words of wisdom, there would be no book*

# Foreword

Dawn's book is a tribute to the enduring heart connection that we form with our beloved animals.
Honoring that connection of love in the way that Dawn has, will give you the courage to listen to your own animals, each in your own special way.

It will encourage others to realize they can be separated from an animal by distance or by death and still feel the connection in their heart as though they were there in the physical form.

It is an honor to write this forward for her book. When she asked me I wanted to know from her what prompted her to write it.

Dawn's answer is so beautiful I want to share it here:
*The book kind of snuck up on me. I was at the field, actually doing TTouch on one of the ponies. Our stable cat (Hero-the subject of the book went outside and there was a lot of commotion). When I went out he had been kicked by one of the ponies. I rushed him to the vet but there was nothing they could do, he was too badly smashed up. I had him put to sleep and brought him home to bury him in the garden. Before I got back he sent me the first poem which I wrote down as soon as I got back. Although nothing like that had ever happened to me before, I knew it was from him. The poems just kept coming. I had bits of paper everywhere. If I tried to change the wording to the way I would have written it, he stopped. It had to be exactly as he gave it to me. It went on for a while and then it was time for him to*

5

*leave. I wasn't sure why he had sent me all of this but when I spoke to the medium she said he wanted people to know that just because our companions are not with us physically, it doesn't mean they are not still beside us. I did try to get it published at the time but had no response and I lost the confidence to pursue it, but I know the time is right now.*

*TTouch has enhanced my life a lot. It has allowed me to help my animals, friends and family and helped with my confidence levels. I know that without it I would not have achieved so much with my ponies, they are very strong characters. Interestingly enough, everyone I have taught uses bent fingers, even though I told them about the different hand positions.*

*I did receive a poem from my favourite horse after I had to have her put to sleep. I was devastated as she was so special. She really did appreciate TTouch; from not being able to touch her at all without being bitten or kicked or squashed, she would stand for hours. We both went off somewhere during the sessions together. Her poem was;*

*Think of me as the wind in the trees,*
*Think of me as the air that you breathe,*
*Think of me as the sun that shines.*
*Think of me and I'll be there,*
*And I'll watch over you,*
*As you watched over me.*

Over the years I have had many experiences that indicate we are never seperated, even when our animals cross the rainbow bridge. I love a statement by author Sylvia Brown, in one of her many books, says she is certain that animals will be waiting for us in heaven. I know that is true because of my experience with the soul retrieval work of Robert Monroe where I have met some of my animals "through the veil."

I realized many years ago that it's possible to ask for proof of that everlasting connection. This realization came when a friend called to say her precious Doberman, Jackson, had died unexpectedly at six years old and she had a feeling of crushing guilt. She believed she had spent too much time working with other people's dogs and neglected her own. She fell into a state of depression and felt that she would never get over the loss and feeling of guilt.

I suggested she communicate with Jackson in a very simple way: sit by his grave, which was in her backyard, and write him a letter - pouring out every thought of pain and guilt and tell him how much she loved him, recalling all the wonderful memories from those six years. Then when she had no more to write she should ask him what he would tell her if he could write to her - and just begin writing. She followed my instructions and was rewarded by words that flowed from her pen from her dog and soothed her heart. I further suggested that when she felt complete she should ask him for a sign to indicate that he was always with her.

This was on a sunny day in July and when she asked for a sign, a miracle happened. For one minute a small cloud formed above the grave, snow fell out of the cloud and covered the spot where her dog lay. Her pain was gone in that minute and she felt his presence in her heart.

I have suggested this process of writing a letter and asking for a return response to many people over the years. Every person has received a reply and felt a sense of completion and deep sense of connection.

Dr. Larry Dossey made a statement in one of his many books that I believe validates this ability to connect with our animals. He wrote: The mind in infinite. My mind touches and is touched by everyones, and all minds are linked.

I believe it is the linking of our infinite minds – all minds and all species – that gives us that deep and lasting connection with a beloved animal. I have been receiving messages from animals and angels and fairies and many forms of nature that have given me a connection to the Oneness of All Being, with Divine Spirit and with All That Is. I would like to share one of them with you:

Reading this sensitive and emotional book will strengthen your belief in interspecies communication, both in the physical and spiritual worlds. Enjoy the journey.

Linda Tellington-Jones, PhD (H)
Founder & President:
Tellington TTouch Training®, Inc

# HERO'S STORY

He arrived at the stables in February 2006 –
starving, sore and very lame.

I didn't expect him to make it for a week, he was
so poorly. But make it he did and he was my
constant companion for 7 months. At times it was
difficult to imagine that he would get better – he
needed lots of TLC, healing, T-Touch and many
homeopathic remedies.

He used to follow me around as best he could and
talked to me most of the time. His favourite time
was teatime – not for the food but the cuddles and
time spent together. Our special time. Luckily,
just before he died, we talked to each other via an
animal communicator. I'm so glad we did.

His departure was sudden, unexpected and brutal.
I was devastated. All the usual emotions – grief,
guilt, anger. His words started to come through
within hours, I knew immediately they were from
him.

I didn't know where his words were leading or
how long they would last, but I just knew I had to
write them all down. Everything is exactly as he
gave it to me – if I tried to change it he wouldn't
give me any more until it was as he said it. The
poems are in the order that they were given to me.

His words really helped me through the difficult times following his death and it was his greatest desire that other people should benefit in their time of grief and loss.

I made him a promise that I would get his poems published and that promise has now been kept.

And so I really hope that you all feel supported and gain some comfort from his words.

Thank you my brave, strong Hero.

I love you so much. Thank you for being a part of my life.

Passed to spirit 30th September 2006

1

## HERO

Hero so brave
Hero so strong
Your time with us was not so long
You stole our hearts with your funny
ways
And helped with love to fill our days
When your time came, much too soon
It was hard to say goodbye
We love you, we miss you
My brave, strong Hero

1

You've left this physical world
And entered the spiritual realm
Where you'll be welcomed with open
arms
Such a kind and gentle soul
Spend lots of time there to
Rebuild and repair
Stay and be happy
And wait for me there

You've left a big hole in my life of my
heart
I wish we were not apart
But I know that the time will come
When we are together again

You are my Hero
Brave and strong
I'm so glad you came along
You filled my heart
With love and care
And asked little in return
A little food, a comfy bed
And cuddles by the thousands
Gentle and kind
Warm and loving
A gentleman in disguise
I welcomed your arrival
I mourn your passing
But when the grief subsides
I will sing your song
Hero the brave, Hero the strong
Just keep marching on

I don't know why you came
I don't know why you went
All I know for certain
You were heaven sent

We tried to help each other
On the rocky bumpy road
It made it so much easier
With you by my side

Now that you have left me
Can I do it on my own?
But when I look around me
I know I'm not alone

You are still there beside me
Just in a different form
So when I ask for guidance
I know just where you'll be

4

Hero my brave soldier
You fell in battle, fatally wounded
I should have protected you but I let you
down
Your enemy was bigger, wouldn't leave
you alone
Your injuries severe, you stood no chance
In your pain and your anguish I was there

As the needle went in
You took your last breath and I was there
I buried you in the safe arms of mother
earth
And I was there
I will always be there with you
And you with me
Hero my brave soldier

5

I couldn't stay in my shattered body
I would suffer too much pain
You knew I wouldn't want it
And so you let me go

Another life, another day
Maybe another form
But we will be together
Of that you can be sure

The bond of love between us
Will guide us on our way
And when we come together
We'll stay a while and pray

This time it will be longer
With time to be alone
But stronger in the silence
Knowing we have each other

In the turmoil of grief
There's no resting place
Every sight and sound
Reminds me of you
It seems so pointless
Why did you go?
Why did you leave me?
I love you so

Your beauty was plain to see
I'm lost without you
I miss you so much
Please come back to me
I look for the signs wherever I go

A sound, a smell, a sight
Is all I require
Just to know you're around
So I can talk to you
To tell you I love you
And I always will

In the darkness of death
No light shines through
I cannot get to you
I know you've gone over
You've gone back home
To rest and recover
My love goes with you
Though my heart feels empty

When will these feelings pass?
They say time heals, I hope that's so
I miss you so, now you had to go
I miss your touch, I miss your presence
My life now feels empty, along with my
heart
I hope in time I'll see that it was meant to
be

That time together, however short
Was enriching for both of our lives
A lesson learned, a love we shared
Count my blessings that we had this time
To love, to learn, to grow

I feel so sad
I feel alone
I've cried and cried and cried
I feel betrayed
You've left me
All on my own
I am so angry
How could you do this to me?

The days are dark, the nights are long
The sun will never shine
I feel so alone and lonely
How could you do this to me?
I don't care about your feelings
I only care about me
Is this how it's meant to be?

In joy and love of light
You're like a shining star
Beaming out the light
For all the world to see
Thank you so much Hero
For choosing to be with me

## 9

Our time together wasn't long
Your passing much too soon
But in our time together
We built a bond so strong
Based on love and trust
It will last forever and still be there
When we are together again

10

Hopefully soon, but maybe not yet
Our pain will go away
But until that time, hold onto the thought
Our love is strong and will endure

## 11

The winds of emotion are raging
Not always what we want
But as the storm is passing
Be quiet and listen
The lesson may be hard
And not one we would choose
But it will speed our passage
What have we got to lose?

Our pain is deep inside us
Can we let it out?
We grieve, we cry, but can we try
To feel the love in our hearts
Don't be bitter or withdrawn
Just be thankful
To have shared some time
With someone we have loved

12

Remember the good times and smile
Remember the bad times and smile
The hurt will fade – the love will not
Be grateful and be honoured

1

Come sit with me and quieten your mind
Be still, be silent and you will hear
The messages I send, for you all of
mankind

Do not be afraid to love, as death can
cause such pain
Love is there is abundance, just to be
claimed
Open up your heart, to love of joy and
peace
Give it freely, do not shrink away
A look, a touch, a thought, all are loving
ways
To express the soul within us as we reach
out to another

You did this for me, I knew you would
That's why I chose you, t'was all in the
plan
To open your heart, to not be afraid

You're nearly there, my job is done
I've given you the key and I'll watch
when you turn it
When you switch on the light I'll rejoice
in its beam
Thank you for caring, for sharing, for
loving
I'll speak to you soon my friend

2

The world of spirit is a wondrous place
Full of love and peace
A place to rest, a place to sleep
A place to think and talk

We meet old friends, long since passed
And freely talk amongst us
A time to reflect on lives just left
Review mistakes and learn from them
Then we can start afresh and not do them
again

We learn new skills, old ones renewed
Enfold them in our soul
When we are ready, there is no rush
We once more incarnate

We remember our source, we remember
our skills
And as we emerge we bring forth love
The gifts we bring are great
For all the world to see
Mother Earth waits for us
With Love of peace and harmony

3

I feel the pain
I feel the blame
It will not go away
Forgive me please dear Hero
Then I can start to heal
I love you, I miss you
My special friend

4

Do not cry
Do not blame
T'was in the master plan
Our time was short
It was meant to be
Rejoice, he happy
Be loved

5

When you are sad and feeling down
Look for me and I'll be there
We shared some time together
We loved each other dearly

I'm no longer in physical form
But that doesn't change a thing
I'll still watch over you
And give you all my love

Don't be sad any longer
Be happy instead
We shared some time together
And soon will again

Speak to me through the seasons
Through the trees and plants and air
Ask me to come
I will always be there

6

I know you're hurt and angry
Because I had to leave
But I am home now
Warm and safe and free
Please be glad for me
I know you find life difficult
Your time to go, not yet
You still have work to do
But I will help you
If you'll let me

I'm here for you
As you were for me
I'll never leave you alone
Have faith, be strong
It won't be long
Your glory time is near

In your darkest hour you came to me
Poor and frail and thin
In your greatest hour you gave your life
With love and light and prayer
Your reason for coming not yet clear
Your reason for going too painful to look
But whatever it was, I thank you
To know you a pleasure
To love you an honour

Let your spirit soar free
Your feet be nimble
My love for your will never dwindle
You touched my life
With love and sparkle
Full of courage and strength
By brave my Hero
By happy my Hero
Above all be who you are
A free and wonderful soul

Where you came from I don't know
But I love you so
You were by my side for not too long
Your time to go too soon
Your sweet and gentle nature
Was plain for all to see
You gave me comfort in times of need
A purr, a smooth, a call, a look
You are so very special
You'll be sorely missed, not just by me
But all who came in contact

You suffered so much in physical form
At the hands of man and beast
But now you're safe
In the arms of angels
So rest now and repair
Fly free great spirit in love and joy
My Hero, my friend, my shining star

11

Your tears are real
Your grief consuming
But take heed
I came to you for a reason
You may not know it now
But time will heal
Then you'll see
It was all in the master plan
So shed your tears
Feel your grief
And then when the sun shines again
Look up and you will see
I'm still here, for you to feel and then you
will heal

Hero my friend, I'm sorry
I let you down in your hour of need
When you were wracked in pain
I should have protected you
But I let it be, I wasn't there for you
If I'd known you were hurt I'd have been
there in a flash
But I didn't and I am sorry

We got to the vets, you were in so much
pain
I couldn't let you suffer
The injuries you sustained were so severe
The outlook was so bleak
I had to let you sleep
If you weren't ready to go I am so very
sorry
I did what I thought best

We brought you home where you wanted
to be
And now you are at peace
Buried with love in the dark of the earth
Your body now redundant
Your spirit is free and unrestrained
To fly and soar and glide
If you fly this way then please feel free
To drop in and visit me
Hero my friend – I love you

They say that time's a healer
I'm not sure that's true
In the depths of my grieving
My loss of you
The strength of my feelings surprised me
You opened up my heart
But now that I have lost you
Is that what I want?
Why couldn't you stay a while and play?
Now that you've gone I feel so alone
But you are free of pain
God bless you Hero, fly away home
But please remember me

14

As I touched your still body
I heard you purr
I waited for you to move
I touched you again – I heard you purr
But still you did not move
I wanted your physical body
But I know it could not be
Your spirit was there
But I could not trust
And so you went away

To wait for the time
When I was ready
To be with you again
I'm trying so hard
To see through the pain
These words I know are coming from you
Our way of contact established
I long for your touch
A sight or a smell
To be with you again

As I buried you in the earth
I couldn't let you go
I didn't want to leave you
Cold and all alone
It's only your physical body
Buried in the soil
Underneath the roses
All out in bloom

16

Know in your heart
It is only the start
Of things you need to know
Grow and learn

17

The road is long
But you're on the way
Fill it with love and joy

18

Look for the good in all you do
Focus on your journey
Never mind the destination
And you path will be easy

Your spirit now is free
To fly and glide and soar
Time now to move on
A new path to follow

20

Do not cry for me
I will cry for you
I am here
You are there
But we are together
I'll see you through your pain
Until we meet again
I'll watch over you

21

The pain you feel is great
It's very hard to bear
Your joy of life had gone
All you feel is loss
I know how much you loved me
I felt it every day
Feel it now within your grief
Bring comfort to your soul

Know that I'm with you all the time
To help you through this time
And when the dark is over
Together we can shine
At times I'll need to leave you
But I'm never far away
Just call and think and I'll be there
Forever by your side

You're in my heart and soul
Forever you'll be there
You're in a different dimension
Now you've left the earthly plane
Our love will keep us together
However far we roam
And one day sweet Hero
We travel together again

I miss your voice
I miss your heartbeat
I miss your silky coat
As you sat on my lap I felt it all
And now you're no longer here
I'm sitting in our place
Of cuddles and love
Awaiting your arrival
I'm so alone
My grief so great
I cannot feel you near
I know you're here
But I feel dead
My heart a heavy burden
Please help me Hero
To feel you again
Your silky coat
Your heartbeat
Your voice
Your love

24

My body is broken
I cannot get in
Please accept me in spirit
And I'll come to you
To guide you and love you
For evermore

Autumn leaves are falling
Gently to the ground
That's where you lie buried
In the arms of Mother Earth
And as your body decays
You feed the soil around you
New life will then emerge

Meanwhile your spirit is free
To grow and sparkle and dance
For all who wish to see

Shine bright my Hero
So you can guide me home
Where we can be together
For all eternity

Your tottering gait
Your hearing dulled
Were all a part of you
And that is why we met
You came to the stables
All hungry and thin
And needed some TLC
You wanted my help
And I gave it gladly

You bore your afflictions with dignity
And never once complained
I know in my heart you wanted change
You battled so hard and it started to ease
But alas it was not to be
Your body failed you at the end
And you were taken from me

I hurt so much
I feel the pain
Of not seeing you again
The loneliness is agony
As I look for you in vain
So please stay close to me
Until I'm strong on my own
Then continue your journey
Wherever it may lead
But please remember to call and visit me

I feel your presence
I know you are here
We've said our goodbyes
On this physical plane
You entered my heart so silently
I didn't know you were there
You live on inside me
Though you're no longer here
And so, till we meet again
Goodbye my Friend
I love you

29

Don't be secretive
Let it all out
Let people know
What you're about
You have the skills
To ease people's ills
Just open up to trust

30

Together as a team
We can touch the stars
And reach into people's hearts
Expose their feelings
For them to see
And watch them clear
With happy glee

## 31

Your soul feeds my spirit
Your beauty feeds my cells
Your purity fills the air
You are a beautiful being
Filled with love and light

32

In the dark of the night
When grief steps in
Think of me and smile
No regrets and don't forget
I'm only a call away

33

My body is redundant
Now that I'm free
But that is all people see
Look beyond – find the spirit
Then you'll really know me

34

Our journey together has just begun
Who knows where it will lead
To the depths of the sea and
Up to the clouds
Just trust and follow me

## 35

I feel you in the wind
I feel you in the sun
I feel you in my bones
Each and every one
Your particles of spirit
Intertwine with mine
Knowing that you're with me
Makes me feel secure

Hero – my friend
I know you're gone
But not for long
Soon we'll be together again
Sharing a life of joy and sorrow
Supporting each other as only friends can
do

37

When things get tough
Too much to bear
Think of me, and I'll be there
As you feel a gentle breeze
Caress your face
You'll know that I am here

38

I watch you lie in troubled sleep
Grieving for my passing
I try to send you messages
It's alright I'm ok
Look at me, I'm free of my body
Maimed and sore
Look at me, I'm free for evermore
No need for guilt or blame or tears
It was meant to be this way

39

Generations ago
I was rich and powerful
But was I happy? – No
I had no love from any source
Life meant nothing
So love it all, every plant every tree
Do it now – just for me

40

Wake up to the wind
Soar in the air
The heavens have opened
To welcome me there

1

When I first met you your flame was
small
In fact it was nearly extinguished
But I gently blew upon your flame
And watched it flicker and grow
I fanned the flame and it got bigger
But only for a while

A big wind came and blew you out
As I sat in the cold and dark of despair
and grief
I suddenly saw a speck of light
I watched in awe as I saw it grow
It got bigger and bigger before my eyes
And there you were

Your light body complete
You sparkled and danced and asked me to
follow
You'd be my guiding star
Bright and warming
Strong and protecting
We followed the path together
Joined in love forever

## 2

As I sit here thinking
What's it all about
Why are we here
On this earthly plane
Do we have choice
Or are we just dumped
Tears of sorrow
Hate and rage
These feelings all around us

We're told we are protected
By our guides and angels
But where are they now?
I can't see them
I can't hear them
I can't feel them
In my grief and despair
I've walled myself up

Perhaps they're out there
Waiting to come in
If I break down the door
Maybe they will enter
But dare I do this
Am I brave enough?
But what if I don't?
I'll be on my own for evermore

I've broken the door
And invited them in

A scary thing to do

As they arrive
So does the light

Now I can see them
Now I can hear them
Now I can feel them

3

My love for you is strong and powerful
It will endure our time apart
And when we are together again
We'll feel it in our hearts

4

My time on earth has ended
It's time for me to go
My work here is finished
So now I must move on

5

Don't torture yourself
With guilt or regret
Conserve your energy for all things good
Love yourself and others too
You're getting the lesson
Hard as it seems
Soon the rewards will be yours

6

Make yourself vulnerable
Learn to trust yourself
And I will guide you
Never fear
I will always be here

7

You think you are weak
But you are strong
And that is why we got along
Your strength is a gift but use it wisely

8

Be quiet and listen
To what I have to say
The negative thoughts you're feeling
Destroy your very soul
And think lighter thoughts
To feed your inner force
Look deep within
See the beauty therein

Hero – I'm not giving you much today, I know you're tired and can't cope.  Don't worry about me, I'm fine, Look after yourself I'm worried about you.  Rest, take your time - there is plenty of time

Me – But I want it now

Hero – And you will get it soon – just be patient

Me – I thought you had deserted me

Hero –You're too tired for much today – take it easy

10

Now that you've left me
You needed to be free
All I have is memories
Of time spent together
You gave me joy
You gave me hope
We gave each other love

11

Sit in the silence and pray
Pray for your salvation
Pray for other people
So they may be healed

12

Follow your dreams
Reach for the stars
I know that you can do it
You'll be a success
It'll be ok
I'll be beside you
Every step of the way

1

I had to go
I know you loved me so
Now that I've left
You feel bereft
Please don't fear
I'm always near
You can hear me
But you can't see me

Your eyes are misted with tears
You can't feel me, stroke my silky coat
You can't reach out, your hands are bent
You can't feel me but I'll be here
I'll wait for things to change
Then when it's time for you to blossom
Reach out, feel, hear, see, touch my silky
coat
But above all, love me

2

Your confidence shattered
Your heart in bits
You feel you can't go on
Take your time, one day at a time
It will all get better
The days are long
The nights are worse
In the silence you have time to think
You mull it over, guilt and blame
All rise to the surface
Could you do it better?
Should you have done it differently?
Would it have made a difference?
The answer to these questions
You really want to know
Go back to silence – listen now
And know that all is well

3

Sing with me
Hear my voice
The time for grief is fading
Time to move along
Take time to smile, to laugh, to cry
In joy and love of life

4

Appreciate life
Make it worth living
Look for the joy and beauty
Tis there is your heart
Though caged at the start
So open the door and on wings of love
Fly free, be open, be loved

5

Let your love shine through
Don't be afraid
Let your light shine brightly
Be who you are
Do not shrink away
Be glad to make a difference

6

I put my hands upon you
The light is coming through
It fills up all your body
Igniting the flame within

7

Life is death
Death is life
It's really all the same
A constantly turning circle
Just like the changing season
So live in the moment
Live life to the full
How long we have, we don't know
Before our time to pass

8

You are me
And I am you
We are one together
Always together
Never apart
Joined by the love in our hearts

## 9

I knew we'd have to say goodbye
But I didn't expect it so soon
My fond memories I'll hold
In my heart forever
Farewell my friend, my love

10

The days are grey and dreary
You have no interest in life
I know the thoughts you're feeling
Since I went away
I only left in physical form
My spirit is still here
Wrapped around you oh so tight
To keep you safe and sound
Please, just look around

## 11

What's it like in leaven
Without your physical body?
Can you run and jump and play?
Is it a place you want to stay?
Please tell me all you know
Then I can rejoice for you
You've found your way back home

12

You live your life so silently
Never letting on
How sad and lonely and lost you feel
I understand it all
But it's time to let go now
Of all the hurt and pain
Ask for help in pastures new
Do not be afraid
I'll hold your hand and gently guide you
The rest is up to you

## 13

Don't cry for me any more
Don't use your energy in grief or regret
Let your tears wash away your sadness
At our sudden parting
Life is for living so enjoy it now
My physical form has left you
My spirit is here instead
Rejoice that we knew and we love each
other
Please be glad that we met

14

Absent friends and ones not met
Give them your love and trust
Some will let you down
But most will love and cherish the gifts
That you bestow on them

15

The material world we live in
Destroys our spiritual growth
We live by others expectations
Really, not our own
So take time now to step away
From all the noise and hype
Be still, be silent, listen to your inner
voice

16

You don't yet know the strength
Buried in your soul
You think you're weak
But you are not
Adversity you've faced
You've struggled long and hard
Your fight is almost over
Your dreams can be achieved.

17

The fields are green
Your heart is black
But light will soon shine through
Don't ponder long on things past
Our bond will always last
I'm in the light, but so are you
If only you could see it

18

Be at peace now
Lay me to rest
Let go of all attachments
Let me go now, we must move on
Our love will always stand the test
Be strong, be brave, be true to you
In time you'll understand
The words I give you now
Take comfort in memories
And savour the time we spent together
We will meet again soon

19

My death to you was brutal
Not fair and ill timed
You saw my shattered body
Lying on the ground
But I was sitting on the fence
I'd already left for home
What you saw was an image
My body in its death throes

When you took me to the vets
I gladly came along
Not in the physical
But in my spirit body
With love and regret you let me go
But cry not, fear not, I am always with
you

The door to my heart is closed
All battered and bruised with pain
At that moment in time
I'm sure I'll never love again
As I sit in the cold darkness of grief
My thoughts in turmoil abound
And yet, I thought I heard a sound
A familiar presence by my side
I think I'm just imagining
Hoping against hope
But I sit in silent expectation
And there it is again
You have not gone
You've just changed form
You're still by my side

## 21

Let your grief run riot
Feel it in every cell
Let it wash all over
Filling all your senses
Until you let this happen
You'll grieve and grieve again
And when the pain subsides
Let love fill all these spaces
Then once more you'll be ready
To open your heart again

In the dark of winter
When the sun doesn't shine
A reflection of the grief I feel
But as winter turns to spring
The light will come in
New growth, new light, new strength
The pain begins to ease
We feel we can go on
In life, in death
We learn the lessons
That we need to know
It isn't always easy
We stumble along the way
When summer arrives
Sun burning bright
We will enter the light

23

As I took my last breath
You were not aware
I wanted it that way
You took good care of me
I wanted to spare you the pain
I knew you would grieve
Your heart would be broken
Your world would fall apart
Don't blame yourself
You couldn't have helped
The pain was quickly gone
When I've recovered and rested
I'll come back to you

24

Remember the good times
Forget the end
Savour our time together
In life you helped me
In death I'll help you
Keep some time for me
In your busy life
Don't forget we all need time to rest
That is when I'll come to you
Our work is ongoing
To help, our aim
Just please listen to ease the pain

25

Never fear
I'll hold you near
A place in my heart forever
I won't forget
Out time together
We shared our mutual love
Keep the space
I'll come again
We'll once more be together

26

In times of change I'll be there
You only have to ask
I recognise your soul
We've travelled together before
This won't be our last meeting
We'll see each other again
I don't know where
I don't know when
But trust me that it will be
Until that time is here
Live in love and joy
I'll be there in spirit
Not in physical form
To help you on your journey
Till we meet again

27

Joyful thoughts
Happy laughter
Be a child again
Be carefree, run and play
You know that I will stay
By your side for ever more
To love and care for you

1

My heart is black
My grief morose
Why did you have to leave?
I thought our time would be so long
Wrapped together, in love so strong
I wish you were here
I miss you so
But my darling
I know you had to go

## 2

We were together for a while
Connected by our love
I loved you
And you loved me
Just the way it was meant to be

3

Live in the silence of heavenly peace
It's here on earth you know
Just look and you will find it
Do not wait for death
And then at your transition
You'll just go through the door

4

With love in your heart
Anything's possible
The way to truth and light
Sorrow should be such a small part
With love in your heart

Your beauty supreme
Your heart magic
You really were the perfect cat
I saw through your afflictions
Twas only make believe
Underneath your silky coat
You were love indeed

6

Listen to your heart
What's it saying to you
Hold on to your grief
Or let it fly way
Don't be angry
Don't be sad
You know it's not for long
In any case, as you well know
I'm only a thought away

7

In the mists of time
With half closed eyes
You will see an image of me
Do not stop it, let it grow
And it will fill your mind
Reminding you of happy times
When we were together
Both in physical form
On the earth plane

8

In physical form I needed no words
You gave me what I needed
Love and affection and more besides
Now that I have left this realm
I need to speak with you
To get across my messages
For all the world to hear
So listen my friend
Be true to me
And you will surely know
That love transcends the great divide
And I will always be
By your side for evermore
For all eternity

I sit here alone
Wondering where you are
You were beside me a way on my journey
But now I must travel alone
In the dark of the night
When I can't see
Please my darling, shine a light for me
I'll follow it gladly
To the end of the road

Your big green eyes
Looked deep inside
And touched my very soul
Our two hearts beat as one
Both of them in tune

11

Do not wait for me
I am already here
I will walk beside you
Whichever path you choose
And I will gently guide you
If you choose to listen

The power of love
There's nothing stronger
It can conquer all
So live in love
Let it light your way
Love not hate
Peace not anger
Acceptance not fear
Live and be love in life

## 13

It's been a little while now
Since you went away
I don't cry so much
I think of you all the time
Need you, miss you, love you
Want you by my side

<u>6th October 2006</u>

1

Our journey now is ending
It's coming to a close
I enjoyed our time together
You gave me care
You gave me hope
You gave me my dignity
You gave your love unconditionally
I'll still be here for you
Just a thought away
But I need to rest and sleep
But I'll be back so soon

2

My words to you are ending
My stories have all gone
Soon you will hear me no more
But don't be sad
Let others hear my words
The bond we have will always last
My true and faithful friend
Let my words spring forth
To let others see
The way it will always be

3

Tis just the start
Of things to come
Of which your part is big
Be strong, be brave
I'm by your side
In the background I'll always be
But it's you
They need to see
To give them hope
To give them love
And turn it all around

I lay in my bed last night
Sad and all alone
Now that you have left me
Here all alone
As I lay in the darkened silence
I suddenly felt you near
You jumped up on the bed
And settled down beside me
You brought a smile to my face
There you stayed all night
Watching over me
You were not there this morning
As I opened up my eyes
I have no fear, I know you're near
And you will come again

5

Please help me see
Your spiritual form
In all its resplendence
How I would love this to be
I know that I can hear you
I'd love to see you
And touch your body once more
If it's meant to be, please help me see
Your beautiful self again

6

In life we were together
And in your death as well
You left me once, I couldn't cope
Do not leave me again
I know I'm being selfish
I don't want you to go
I hear your words
They make me strong
I want to hear them always
In the silence without them
What will I do?

Please stay a bit longer
If you can
And stay and talk to me
I'll listen hard
Your words impart
The way you asked me to
But please not yet
Do not leave me again
I really am not ready
Maybe soon but not today
I really need you so

I sit in the silence of grief
Awaiting the answers that I seek
The questions not yet formed
Please help me my friend
Why did you go?
Where are you now?
What are you doing?
Are you in heaven?
What's it like?
Is it as they say it is?
A place to rest, a place to play?
Is there a heaven on earth?
Or it is just an illusion?
I need to know, please help me so
So I can feel the peace once more
And let you go in love

If ever there was a beautiful being
It was you
Quiet and unassuming
Your light shone through
You battled on determinedly
With courage, strength and grace
But when you end came suddenly
Your body melted away
And I found the missing piece
Your soul was oh so bright
A guiding shining light
For everyone to see

You've left your physical form
Your spirit now floats free
You do not need your body
You left it all behind
My memories of you I'll hold
Deep within my heart
And for the time that we're apart
I'll love and treasure these

11

Let go of your anger
Let go of your rage
Accept your resentment
Just let it fade

12

Remember the good times
Let them fill your heart
You have your memories
While we spend time apart

## 13

Do not cry in grief
It's too painful
For you and for me
Laugh instead
Live life to the full
Do not cry in grief for me
Cry in love instead

15

Wrapped in your arms
You kept me safe and warm
Enclosed in my heart
Is your love and care
I'll do the same for you
In any way I can
So just please remember
Reach out and I am there

## 16

In our grief
We seek the peace
Of knowing that you cared
And of the love we shared
We know you had to leave us
It was surely time to go
But please my friend
Remember us
And send us all your love

## 17

In the quiet and the stillness
I no longer hear your voice
I wish it could be different
I wonder if I imagined it
The words I heard you say
But I know that it was you
Messages of love and sympathy
For you and me and all
I know this is the last one
At least for a little while
So go in peace my friend
I'm glad I loved you so

# Conversation

Me:I can't take this one cos I know that's it

Hero:You have to, please

Me:I don't want to lose you again

Hero:You haven't but I'm tired now, I need to rest.  If I give you any more the meaning will be lost

Me:I wish you weren't going, it really helps to hear you.  Please try to let me see you, it will really help me

Hero:OK I'll try

Me:Will you be back to talk to me?

Hero:Maybe, but not yet

Me:Thank you so much Hero, I love you

Hero:I know, I love you too

18

I know that you can hear me
Wherever you have gone
I thank you for your loving words
I thank you for our meeting
Now I'll let you rest in peace
My dear sweet Hero
Sleep and rest and heal

## 7th October 2006

1

Do not look for me
For I am by your side
In life, in death I came to you
But then I had to leave

I didn't think it was time to go
I really wanted to stay
To feel your love
Your healing hands
But alas it was not so
Be pleased my friend
You let go with love

2

I've found my friends
They welcomed me back
We run and jump and play
I can be here
I can be there
I can be just anywhere
So look for me wherever you may be

## 12th October 2006

1

Don't grieve for me my friend
I had to move along
Our time together wasn't that long
Together we walked the path of life
If only for a while
Joined in love and trust

2

Don't think of me with sadness my friend
Think with joy instead
Remember happy time spent together
You with me
And me with you
Sitting in the silence
Of quiet solitude

3

Think of me with love my friend
And watch me spread my wings

## 4

My dear sweet Hero
I feel your anger
I sense your discord
Why?
You know you had to go
Perhaps you didn't want to leave
Me here alone
I couldn't come
My time's not done
You have to go alone
The decision was made long times ago
The truth in that you know
I give you my heart
I give you my love
I wrap you in joy and grace
And so my dear sweet Hero
Go in love and joy and grace
Go and find eternity

5

I see you sitting quietly
Waiting for my words
But they are more difficult now
For me to send to you
I want to stay
I need to go
I am all in conflict
I'm here in spirit
Yet bound to the earth plane
We still have work to do
Listen hard and help me
While I sort this problem out
Be pleased to hear me
But do not miss me
If I have to go

1

Listen to the words I speak
For I bring the truth to you
Heaven on earth
Earth in heaven
Tis really all the same

We still live amongst you
Just in a different dimension
If only you could see through the veil
That separates our two worlds

You would see the love, the beauty, the
joy
That abounds in this wonderful place
Then you would be so happy for us
To be in this peaceful place
Where we can rest, recover and grow

It only needs a thought
To bring us by your side

So think of us often
And call us with love
We will be there

1

It's OK
I can finally let go
It's time for me to move on
You let me go
With love and compassion

It really helps you know
To cut the ties
Of this earthly plane
And move to different dimensions

One day soon, but not just yet
I'll talk with you again
To bring you words of wisdom
To bring you words of truth

Remember me with love
Treasure your memories
I know that you loved me, oh so much
Just as I loved you
But be glad for me
Cradled in the arms of unconditional love

1

Just rest a while with me
Take time out to play
Just listen to the words of guidance
That will come your way

You don't have to strive
Just sit back
You will see
Just be quiet
Just be still

Allow your mind to still
Your guides are waiting patiently
With words of wisdom and love
They really want to help you
But you need to let them in

You have work to do
And they'll help you all they can
But be still
Just be

The words will come
At times too fast
For you to understand
Be patient, listen and you will fully know
The path you need to follow

Lightning Source UK Ltd.
Milton Keynes UK
UKOW05f1150240714

235688UK00001B/1/P